Pulling the Wolf

Out of the Sheep

An Entrepreneur's Quick Guide

Book and Workbook

Cassandra Mouton

AN ENTREPRENEUR'S QUICK GUIDE

Copyright © 2016
Cassandra Mouton
All rights reserved.

ISBN-10: 1542603803
ISBN-13: 978-1542603805

COPYRIGHT 2016
ALL RIGHTS RESERVED

NO PART OF THIS PUBLICATION MAY BE REPRODUCED, STORED IN A RETRIEVAL SYSTEM, OR TRANSMITTED IN ANY FORM OR BY ANY MEANS, ELECTRONIC, MECHANICAL, PHOTOCOPY, RECORDING, OR ANY OTHER, WITHOUT THE PRIOR PERMISSION OF THE AUTHOR.

CASSANDRA MOUTON

To

From

AN ENTREPRENEUR'S QUICK GUIDE

Acknowledgments

Special thanks to:

Cover Design: Geisy Rivas
Interior Design: BY Publishing
Editor: Rachelle M. Clark
Production Management:
A&D Management, LLC

CASSANDRA MOUTON

DEDICATION

I dedicate this first book to my family. Without you, I would not be the woman I am today. To my mother, Delores, for the many sacrifices she has made to make sure I never went without, and always giving me wise and unbiased advice. To my brother, Terrance, for always protecting me, teaching me to be tough, and always pushing me to be great. To my sister, Sandra, for having a listening ear and having my back at all times. To my father, Leroy, for being the first man to ever love me. To my best friend, Anthony, for always allowing me to cry on his shoulders, helping me to get back up when I feel like I can't, for always understanding and accepting me, and most importantly, for always sharing gut busting laughter. To my late grandparents, and extended family: thank you for your support, always encouraging me to do my best, and loving me unconditionally. I love you all from the bottom of my heart.

AN ENTREPRENEUR'S QUICK GUIDE

THANK YOU

Special thank you to my church family and childhood friends. Thank you for your continued love and support. Thank you to my work family and mentors for helping and guiding me on my journey, and creating memorable moments with me. Thank you to my friends who contributed to this book, I truly appreciate your support.

Most importantly, I thank God for creating, trusting and using me to be a light.

Lastly, thank you for supporting me and allowing me to share my first book with you.

CASSANDRA MOUTON

TABLE OF CONTENTS

WHY THIS BOOK	9
GETTING TO KNOW ME	11
INTRODUCTION	13
THE BEGINNING, BEFORE THE BEGINNING	15
LESSON 1: IDENTIFYING YOUR TRUE SUPPORTERS	16
Workbook and Activities	19
LESSON 2: LEAP OF FAITH	22
Workbook and Activities	25
LESSON 3: CONFIDENCE	30
Workbook and Activities	33
LESSON 4: SKILLS	37
Workbook and Activities	40
LESSON 5: SPEAK UP, HAVE A VOICE	43
Workbook and Activities	45
LESSON 6: IDENTIFYING WOLVES	48
Workbook and Activities	52
LESSON 7: GUIDING NEW SHEEP	56
Workbook and Activities	59

LESSON 8: GUT CHECK 59

       Workbook and Activities 63

LIVING IN YOUR PURPOSE 65

FINAL WORDS OF ADVICE 67

ABOUT THE AUTHOR 70

NOTES 72

ABOUT BY PUBLISHING ....--............. 84

CASSANDRA MOUTON

WHY THIS BOOK

The world is full of sheep and wolves. What would you identify yourself as: a sheep, a wolf, or both?

These animals have distinctive characteristics that distinguishes them from one another, and whether it's in life or in business, you are one of them. At heart, I am a sheep. Everyone who meets me can see and feel that about me; and I never really thought that I needed to be a certain way in order to be successful in business. But as I began my entrepreneurial journey, I had a few people pull the wolf out of me. I knew that it was there, but I didn't expect for it to be forced out. Don't get me wrong, I am still a sheep. However, now I have a better understanding of when the wolf in me is necessary.

I had a conversation with my brother once and as he listened quietly, I gradually began to witness the wolf in him come out. He has always been protective over me, and if there's anyone that can prevent someone else from hurting or taking advantage of me, it's him.

He explained, and also reminded me, about the world of business and how there are sheep and wolves within it. The sheep are eaten by the wolves if the wolves are able to roam freely amongst them without set boundaries. If the sheep cannot adjust, they will not survive.

His explanation and scenarios made perfect sense. I needed to pull out the wolf in me in order to survive and "make it" in life and in business. I've learned that it's okay to care; but not okay to let others take advantage of you without speaking up for yourself. It's not okay to allow others to discredit or steal your work, and it's certainly not okay to let them disrespect or belittle you. Once he explained how sheep and wolves operate, I finally *got* it; the wolf was in me, but I often hid it.

CASSANDRA MOUTON

GETTING TO KNOW ME

I am an extremely caring and giving woman. Oftentimes, I am lending a helping hand, cheering someone on to greatness, or offering assistance along the way. I am the one who remains calm when everyone and everything around me is chaotic and dysfunctional. I am the one people come to when there is a problem or if they need a listening ear or sound advice. I am the one who may appear to be selfoccupied and lost in her own thoughts, yet has actually observed and taken note of everything that was said and done. I may not say much, but best believe I'm taking mental notes. Without question, I will give my very last or even half of what I have.

I also don't mind causing a stir, although, growing up my mother often told me to be quiet and to not get involved. I try to keep my emotions in check, therefore I internalize them; but once I've reached a certain point of suppression, that's when the wolf begin to surface. Once this happens, I no longer care for your feelings or about being silent- I'm coming for you. I guess you can say that's the Scorpio in me too, but thankfully I am able to keep that side of me under control.

If you come at me incorrectly, I'll no longer bite my tongue or grant seconds chances. I will come for you, but only to get my point across. I will not be mean, because I'm a lady and my mama raised me to be respectful and polite; but trust me, you will feel me one way or another. Sometimes I have to talk the wolf away, because I can feel the rage inside of me, wanting to destroy and go for blood. Of course I mean this figuratively, but you get the point.

I may not physically or verbally do anything to harm you, but my silence can kill and my moves will make you regret you were ever against me. Afterwards, I begin to laugh as the wolf calmly cuddles back up on the inside, napping until an ignorantly-determined individual nudges it to return. I haven't had to unleash the Scorpion yet, however, the wolf in me has made its mark and ready to take a stand whenever necessary.

CASSANDRA MOUTON

INTRODUCTION

I've always wanted to start my own business, because I've never really liked people telling me what to do, when and how to do it, where to go, who to meet, etc. I absolutely hate it. Just show me what it is that you need me to do, let me take my notes so that I can practice, and leave me be. Shall I find a way to do the job more quickly, accurately, and on point, then let me do so. I don't need you breathing your hot, stinky breathe down my neck while I'm trying to work- not that I don't need the extra support at times, but *dang*, let me breathe. If I make a mistake, allow me to correct it. I don't need a long, drawn out speech or lecture about everything under the sun, especially when it doesn't pertain to anything regarding my actual work.

Yes, I have a "smart mouth" but I often keep such comments to myself. Sometimes these kind of remarks tend to slip out and other times it's purposefully done so that ears can hear. I say a lot through my facial expressions, although, I haven't been able to master the art of poker face yet. I often laugh internally when I know my face tells the truth of what I am thinking. More than likely, the individuals taking offense to my *you'refull-of-shit-poker-face* are the ones who truly deserve it in my book.

Don't judge me, because I don't claim to be perfect. I am perfectly flawed. I am somewhere between introvert and extrovert- more so an introvert- therefore, for those who do not know me or understand my internal struggles, find it more difficult to relate and empathize with. My best friend says I'm a "social turtle", which I explain in my other book: Entrepreneur's Quick Guide to Team Building.

Part of the reason I chose to write this book was because although I have a lot of introverted ways, I am also an entrepreneur. Many people doubted that I could pull this off because I've never written a book before, don't always articulate my words correctly, don't have the gift of gab, didn't attend a prestigious school, prefer not to have small talk with strangers, and I don't pretend to be someone that I am not.

But as always, I proved them wrong. Who is them, you may ask? They are all of the "haters" and doubters who never supported me, yet are wondering how I became successful. I observe them patiently waiting to hear the latest gossip about me, lurking to see what's new on my social media accounts, searching to see something negative about me. But as always, they find nothing.

CASSANDRA MOUTON

THE BEGINNING, BEFORE THE BEGINNING

My best friend always laughed at me and told me to hurry up and start my own business, because I will probably get fired from someone else's place of employment. He would shake his head as I vented about my superiors and their complaints about me being nonchalant. My superiors would always say I had a look on my face as if I was saying, "shut the heck up" or "you don't know jack". My best friend knows my thoughts so well and the meaning behind all of my facial expressions, which is quite hilarious. We stay laughing all of the time, knowing that one day, someone may actually fire me because of these things.

I crack myself up and some people may not understand my humor, but that's okay. I will continue to be me.

I knew working towards being an entrepreneur would be a challenge, but I never thought the people I looked up to as mentors, could be some of the best and worst people to help me along the way. I'm not suggesting that everyone has ill intentions, but once someone shows you who they really are, you better believe them. This is not only applicable to entrepreneurs or business professionals, but to people in general- even family members and the folks who consider themselves a real friend.

LESSON 1: IDENTIFYING YOUR TRUE SUPPORTERS

I had a "friend" who said they were going to help me. As long as I was doing what they wanted me to do, everything was good. As long as they had the upper hand while getting the most out of the relationship, everything was great. This also pertains to daily relationships. See, as long as you are giving the most in the relationship and the other person is constantly taking, without investing much back into the relationship, they are good. But the moment you say something, or even began to take a little bit of their time or benefits away, it becomes a problem.

How is this beneficial to you? How is this nurturing and building the relationship? If a relationship is only one sided or if you're constantly giving yet hardly ever receiving anything in return, then that is a problem. It's just like a bank- if you are constantly taking money out of the account, but never depositing anything back into it, then it will eventually overdraft.

Those so called "friends" or "business partners" are not what they appear to be; they are leeches, sucking the life out of you. They are draining you financially, mentally, emotionally, and physically. If they have managed to drain you in any way, especially spiritually, then *stop* and distance yourself immediately.

These types of people don't care that they haven't contributed to the relationship. They don't care about the toll it is taking on you, your health, your finances, or the sacrifice you are making for them. They don't care that you have been giving everything in the relationship and haven't received much in return. All of that doesn't matter to them because they are selfish and not a real friend. Just as in any healthy and loving relationship, it's a give and take situation.

Having your own business and being your own boss is hard work, yet rewarding at the same time. You will definitely have to sacrifice in order to get ahead. A guy once told me that in order to be successful in having your own business, you have to give up what you love. I haven't quite figured that out though, because I don't feel like I have given up anything just yet.

The main thing that comes to mind is the decrease and uncertainty of income when starting your own business. It's scary, because you no longer have that security blanket of working for someone's' else business, which oftentimes guarantee a steady income and insurance. If you are able to work somewhere for a steady income while balancing your own business, then do that. If not, then go hard or go home because you will be putting in hours of work into your business which may or may not pay off immediately.

I never make a business move unless I know I have my family support. I don't have to ask their permission or anything like that because I know they have my back. I told them what I wanted to do and they knew I was going to pursue it, with or without them. I didn't need their financial or physical help, just emotional support. If I failed and needed to be bailed out, I knew I could count on them and my best friend for help. Although everyone's family members are not as supportive, I am very grateful to have my immediate family and best friend's support with whom I know will sacrifice for me if necessary, and vice versa.

AN ENTREPRENEUR'S QUICK GUIDE

Lessons and Assignments

Lesson 1: Identifying Your True Supporters

Who are your Supporters and how are they depositing into your life and/or business?

_____

_____

_____

_____

_____

_____

_____

_____

_____

_____

Who are your drainers and what are they taking from you? People who take away from you and constantly want/need something.

_____

_____

_____

Who are you supporting and depositing into? How are you doing it?

_____

_____

Assignment: Set boundaries and know what you are willing to accept and not accept

Assignment: Once you have identified your supporters and drainers, get rid of or limit your time and energy to your drainers.

LESSON 2: LEAP OF FAITH

Two years ago, I took a leap of faith in the world of entrepreneurship. I had a plan, but that plan did not play out the way I had hoped; so I decided to focus on entrepreneurship full time. It made sense for me to take that step, because I didn't want to work for anyone anymore. And as I previously mentioned, I didn't like others telling me what to do and when to do it. I prefer making the rules up as I go. So far, it has been a crazy journey; some lessons have been learned and others I haven't quite grasped yet, but I am confident it will all come together.

What exactly do people mean when they say take "a leap of faith"? I mean, can they help you pay your bills when the money is no longer coming in? Can they pay your medical bill if something tragic happens to you since you quit your job? Can they direct you towards the right path, because taking a leap of faith doesn't come with instructions? Well, in my case, I took a leap with no road map.

I knew the direction I wanted to go and the results I wanted to see, but I had absolutely no clue about how to get there. The paths I thought were the right one to take were only lessons I endured along the way. Sometimes you have to go through a few things that are to prepare you for the journey. It's not a mistake that you end up at a dead end; you just didn't realize which turn to make. Sometimes you come to a dead end because you were supposed to switch paths along the way, yet did not.

Furthermore, each move you make will always lead you to where you are meant to be. Most will take shorter, easier paths, while only a few are willing to endure long, bumpy, and difficult ones.

I don't look at this journey as me starting over, but more so as my transition to greatness. It's taking longer than expected, but in due time everything will fall into place- much like a puzzle. When it's the right piece, it will interlock perfectly amongst the rest, which is in contrast to those that often get stuck, will not fit, and obviously don't belong.

When to Take the Leap

If you are wondering if you should take a leap of faith or even when, look no further. When you have prayed about it and God tells you to move. Or whoever your spiritual beliefs have you to pray to.

I spent many nights and days in crying sessions with God, asking for a way out of my current misery. I wanted to help others, but not how I started out doing it. I wanted to make a difference in the world. I wanted to be my own boss. I didn't want to be in the spotlight, but I knew I wanted to be behind the scenes. I wanted people to hear so many great things about me, so much that when they finally meet me, they would be amazed. I wanted them to be surprised. I loved the feeling I got when someone finally got to see who was actually behind all the work.

I received several spiritual confirmations before actually taking that leap. It was constantly on my mind. All of a sudden, I began to overhear people speak about specific instances during the same time that I was questioning God. Opportunities began to present themselves, but of course the first couple of times I did not act on them.

Then God said, "Okay. You're not moving when I'm telling you to move. You're not taking the opportunities I am giving you."

When you ask God for something and expect Him to deliver, yet you don't move when He commands you to, He will begin shaking things up to the point where you will become less content and comfortable. He will lay it upon your spirit and you will not be able to get rid of it; and sometimes He will switch things up on you so that you have no choice *but* to move.

Some people straddle the fence when it comes to being a business owner- only wanting to take the leap with one foot out, keeping the other one on safe grounds. I mean, it's understandable that you want to make sure you have the financial security to take care of your responsibilities, but you also have to trust and believe that it will all work itself out. Some people are able to internalize that, but most aren't.

Lessons and Assignments

Lesson 2: Leap of Faith

What are the things that are holding you back from taking the leap of faith?

_____

_____

_____

_____

_____

_____

_____

_____

_____

Have you thought of a plan if you take that leap? What is it?

_____

_____

_____

_____

Do you pray/meditate daily for guidance? What do you need guidance on?

What are you afraid of?

_____
_____
_____
_____
_____
_____
_____
_____
_____

How are you preparing for your leap?

_____
_____
_____
_____
_____

What is something that constantly tugs at your heart and stays on your mind?

Assignment: Make a list of what you want to accomplish. Place it in a safe place such as your bible, jewelry box, etc. and read it out loud to yourself regularly.

Assignment: Pray/meditate and ask for daily guidance.

AN ENTREPRENEUR'S QUICK GUIDE

LESSON 3: CONFIDENCE

Having confidence in yourself is a must. If you don't have confidence in yourself, then who will? If you have to "fake it until you make it", then that's what you do. If you don't know how to do that, then I'll share something you *can* do.

I have always been confident and the times I weren't, no one knew with the exception of my best friend and immediate family. I didn't have to tell them that I wasn't sure of myself, because they could already sense it. I didn't have to "fake it" with them and even if I tried, they would eventually see past the facade.

In my adolescence, I can recall that moment when two of my friends' mothers approached me. They praised me, saying how proud they were of me and how they wish their daughters had the confidence I had. They complimented my way of dress, attitude, ability to talk to others with ease, and willingness to adjust to any situation without getting flustered. I didn't think much of it at the time, but this example shows how others are always paying attention to your character, even when you don't know it. You should always carry yourself in a respectable and confident manner. You never know who might be encouraged, inspired, and motivated by your actions, even when you feel inadequate. It is always important to seek help if you are struggling with your self-esteem or selfworth, because this can directly affect your level of confidence and incur self-doubt.

Things to Do and Remember to Build Confidence

Speak positive affirmations to yourself on a daily basis; say them in the mirror, write them down, and post them throughout your house. Remind yourself how great you are.

Set small attainable goals you want to accomplish that will contribute to the big picture and plan.

Dress for success. If you look the part then you will start believing it and the rest will follow.

Start an exercise regimen or take time to meditate. *De-clutter* your mind and *de-stress*. Breathe in deeply through your nose and exhale out through your mouth.

Make time for yourself by doing something you enjoy. Participate in an activity, engage in a hobby, get a massage, or take a road trip.

Take time to pat yourself on the back. If you don't do it, who will?

March to your own beat and sing to your own tune. Don't allow others to control your thoughts and actions. Do what you feel is right.

It's okay to have an "off" day. Just get back up and continue to grind it out.

Identify and learn from your mistakes and failures. Never give up and continue to improve yourself.

Avoid negative people.

Research and gain knowledge to perfect your craft. You will be more confident speaking to others about what it is that you do.

Don't be afraid to ask for or recieve help. It's better to get an understanding of something rather than to be ignorant to it.

No matter what, stay positive and optimistic. Your hard work will pay off in the end.

Take it a day at a time; this will not be a quick fix. It takes time to build yourself up.

Don't over-book, over-stretch, or take on more than you can handle. Stress comes with the territory, but it doesn't have to consume your life.

Have the courage to walk away and start over if and whenever necessary.

AN ENTREPRENEUR'S QUICK GUIDE

Lessons and Assignments

Lesson 3: Confidence

What are your weaknesses?

_____
_____
_____
_____
_____
_____
_____
_____
_____
_____

What are your strengths?

_____
_____
_____
_____

What are some things you can do to build your confidence?

When have you felt the most confident?

_____

_____

_____

_____

_____

_____

_____

_____

When have you felt inadequate and less confident?

_____

_____

_____

_____

_____

_____

_____

_____

_____

_____

Assignment: Make a list of things you need to work on to help boost your self-esteem and confidence?

Assignment: List 3 short term goals that will contribute to the big plan and do them within 1-3 months.

AN ENTREPRENEUR'S QUICK GUIDE

LESSON 4: SKILLS

Being an entrepreneur is scary. The world is not going to just hand you everything you want and need. Sometimes you may not even know what you are doing, how you are going to do it, or how you are going to make it work. Sometimes you'll have absolutely no clue on what your plan is.

However, it *is* important to know what you are good at before you decide to be an entrepreneur. For some, it may not be that easy to declare your strengths until you just dive in and do it. For myself in particular, I didn't know what I was good at, and therefore, I definitely had no idea who my clientele would be. I was good at many things so I never truly mastered one specific skill set. To be honest, I didn't think I needed to do so- and still don't- but I will acknowledge that I should focus on each skill individually in order to make it great. Most people only focus on what they're good at, but there are a few people like myself who happen to be good at everything all around. Although, I hope I'm not tooting my horn prematurely.

Investments

Nurture your craft and skill. In order to become great at something you must first take time to perfect it. There are many resources out there that can help you become better, so be willing to invest in yourself. Nowadays, you have the option to read books, go online, watch videos, listen to tapes, podcasts, and attend informative events. In the beginning, you probably won't have the finances to invest in yourself or your business, however, that shouldn't stop you from investing *time* into nurturing your passions.

Although you may not have the finances, you can gain access to free educational videos online through YouTube for example, and free seminars that are provided through various agencies. There are plenty of great profit and non-profit companies who provide free workshops, business resources and counseling such as Score, U.S. Small Business Administration, local libraries, and community colleges to name a few.

Investing will cost you time, money, or both. If you don't have the money, then invest the time- and vice versa. Don't be afraid to volunteer at an event so that you may get the information you need to deposit into your business. Whether you have to work the registration table, help desk, or assist with seating arrangements, that doesn't matter. What matters most is that you are in the right place to get the information you need. Feel free to mingle and network with other volunteers who also have likeminded business goals; this doesn't require any money out of your pocket.

Along with financial investments, comes sacrifice. Eventually, you will have to sacrifice your time, but temporarily, you can pay someone to do the work for you. With this, there are many investors, consultants, and workers who are willing to assist and help you build your dream business.

So, if you are spending your own money, you definitely want to make sure it is going to the right places.

Lessons and Assignments

Lesson 4: Skills

What do you enjoy doing?

_____

_____

_____

_____

_____

_____

_____

_____

_____

What skill(s) can you focus on to make great?

_____

_____

_____

AN ENTREPRENEUR'S QUICK GUIDE

_____

_____

_____

_____

_____

_____

_____

What are some resources in your town you can get information from?

_____

_____

_____

_____

_____

_____

_____

_____

_____

Who can you follow on social media to get free business advice, knowledge, and motivation?

_____

_____

_____

_____

_____

_____

_____

_____

_____

_____

Assignment: Identify 3 workshops, seminars, or meetings to go to (free or a price you can afford) and attend?

Assignment: Identify 3 networking opportunities to attend (not your usual networking group)

LESSON 5: SPEAK UP, HAVE A VOICE

Speak with authority.

I am so quick to defend others, yet hesitant to speak up for myself which indirectly causes others to misjudge or take advantage of my kind spirit.

Actually, let me retract my statement.

I *do* speak up for myself, however, I often "let things slide" or give it no attention until it begins to irritate or affect me; but by this point, it's time for me to put those things back in its proper place.

But that's something I have to work on more. I'm learning that as quick as I am to stand up for others, I should be just as quick to stand up for myself. Speak up for yourself, even if that means no one has your back.

Don't allow others to take you out of character. If you don't speak up, then people will think they can treat you any kind of way. Because of this, they are more liable to disrespect and take advantage of you.

How to Have a Voice

If you need time to get your thoughts together, take as many moments necessary to think things through.

Write down what you think and feel. You can always piece it together.

Make notes and bullet points to help you stay on track and address all of your issues.

Be stern, but respectful and tactful.

Know the facts.

Do not speak based off of your emotions alone.

Listen.

AN ENTREPRENEUR'S QUICK GUIDE

Lessons and Assignments

Lesson 5: Speak up: Have a voice

What is something you need to speak up more about?

_____
_____
_____
_____
_____
_____
_____
_____
_____
_____

Who are you afraid to speak up to and why?

_____
_____
_____
_____

_____

_____

_____

_____

_____

_____

_____

What's your plan of action to address your challenges?

_____

_____

_____

_____

_____

_____

_____

_____

_____

Assignment: Write down your thoughts and feeling about any challenges you are facing. Once that is complete, make bullet points.

Assignment: Write down possible solutions and barriers to the challenges you are facing. Now address it.

LESSON 6: IDENTIFYING WOLVES

What comes to mind when you think of a sheep and a wolf? What are their characteristics? What type of relationship do they have with one another?

Gaining the proper knowledge about sheep and wolves is important, not only in business, but life in general. I have met many people who have taught me valuable lessons by helping me pull the wolf out of myself. Neither of your experiences with a wolf or sheep are invaluable. You will either learn from it, make a new friend through it, or gain access to additional resources and networks to help you reach your goal.

The Manipulator

This type of person may befriend you and find ways to use said friendship against you. Oftentimes, you may not even realize that you are being manipulated, because this person knows all the right things to say, in such a way to convince you to do what they want. Although this is true, pay close attention to *what* they say, *how* they say it, and what they *do*. Observing their actions is a major key to figuring out if manipulation is taking place. Sometimes, this person may appear to be understanding or offering their help, but in reality, they are only interested in finding more ways to benefit from you.

If you call them out on their bullshit, they'll likely become upset and attempt to their process of manipulation in other ways. If they have leverage over you, trust me, they will use it. Whether it's through finances, information, or resources, they will attempt and threaten to take any of these things away to keep you under their control. They will try to make you believe that you need them and can't do it without them. They enjoy giving you a false sense of hope or even doubt.

One wolf tried to convince me that I wasn't ready to start my own business and to *not* take that leap of faith. He always made it appear as if he had my best interest at heart, expressing that he "wanted to protect me from the mean world of business."

This is similar to a romantic relationship. When you are fed up and ready to walk away, they know just what to say or do to make you stay. They manipulate you into staying, not moving forward, because they want to be in control of the situation; sabotaging your moves so that you continue to move in their favor.

The Asshole

Assholes are rude and disrespectful to others on so many levels, whether it's with their words or actions. They make you want to punch them in the mouth or even the eye. Their smart, swift remarks makes you question why they are even in your presence.

Many assholes know they are assholes and enjoy making others feel uncomfortable. They purposely do things to jeopardize your business and your brand by spreading rumors, lacking tactfulness, and having no shame in being downright wrong. They want to assist you in failing so that they can stand around, talk crap, throw dirt, and kick you while you're down so that they can feel better about themselves. Yet, little do they know, their actions won't give them true power, just Karma- and you know she is a *beast*.

The Bully

Everyone knows, or has known, a bully once in their lifetime. This type of person enjoys embarrassing others through physical, mental, and emotional abuse. They are completely insecure and believe that by treating others with disrespect and aggression, it will make them likeable.

This is so far from the truth.

Everyone won't be capable of standing up to their bully, because oftentimes they are afraid and every bully is different. A wolf-bully lacks self-confidence in their life, so they attempt to intimidate those around them that are quiet and less likely to defend themselves. Very seldom will you see a bully attack someone that is confident and speaks up for themselves and others.

The Big Brother/Sister

I consider my brother one of the good guys. Not only do I say that because he is my brother, but mainly because he is a successful business owner. He is protective and encouraging, but also tells me the things that I need to hear- even when I don't want to hear it. He doesn't sugarcoat anything or make me believe something is a certain way, when it is not.

The big brother or sister doesn't mind guiding you and taking you under their wing. They are supportive and willing to help you make it to the top if they see you putting in your best work efforts. They believe that when *you* win, *they* win, and vice versa. They teach you how to keep your business and personal life separate.

The Pushover

The pushover is a sheep pretending to be a wolf. These sheep have not learned to stand up for themselves and instead, allow others to make decisions for them- even if it's not in their best interest. The pushover hasn't found their voice yet, therefore, in order to walk away unbothered, they go along with everyone else to keep the peace. They might be in leadership positions, but their actions speak differently.

Lessons and Assignments

Lesson 6: Identifying wolves

What types of wolves are in your life?

_____

_____

_____

_____

_____

_____

_____

_____

_____

_____

What type of wolf are you or would like to be and why?

_____

_____

_____

_____

_____

_____

_____

_____

_____

Assignment: Identify people in business who are wolves and sheep. Be sure to have someone represent each wolf. List the pros and cons of each on how they do business.

Assignment: If you are not the wolf you would like to be, what are some steps you can take to become that? Now start working on them.

LESSON 7: GUIDING NEW SHEEP

As an entrepreneur, it's important to share your knowledge of business so that others may become successful in their own way. People have been taught to believe that if someone else becomes successful, then it will take away from their own success.

This is not true.

Who's to say that the person you are helping, wants anything to do with what you do? Who's to say that there isn't room at the top for everyone?

Don't be stingy with your gifts and talents. Someone took the time to teach and nurture you into the person you are. So, be thankful for that. Even if they were not one hundred percent supportive of your dreams, that helped you. I'm not saying its okay to be that way with others, but just think back on how you started and all the challenges you faced. As business owners, we are able to identify and connect with one another in some way, so why wouldn't you want to help the next person? Why wouldn't you want to pour knowledge and positivity into the next person?

Mentors

Everyone needs a mentor, even if they are not in the same industry as you. It doesn't have to be just one either, you can have many. For me, the mentors in my life are other successful business owners and those who are making a difference in the lives of others.

A friend once told me that he spends as much time as possible with his friends who are millionaires. Not because he is looking for a handout, but because they are able to share the lessons they've learned thus far and give sound advice. As a result of this mentor-mentee relationship, he now has access to some of the things that he may not have had, if it strictly stemmed from his own resources. He admires their businesssavvy habits and tries his best to imitate those same characteristics. This is a real life example of what happens when you practice better habits on a daily; they will eventually become imbedded in your DNA.

Lessons and Assignments

Lesson 7: Guidance

Do you have a mentor? Who are they?

_____

_____

_____

_____

_____

_____

_____

_____

_____

_____

What things are your mentors pouring into you and have it been beneficial or harmful to you and your business?

_____

_____

_____

Have you started to pour into others? If so, what have you been providing and have you seen that person flourish because of it?

_____

_____

Assignment: If you have not linked up with someone who can be a mentor to you, identify at least 5 people or attend places where you can locate them.

Assignment: What things would you like to get from your mentor? Discuss your vision and allow them to invest their time guiding you with what they have.

AN ENTREPRENEUR'S QUICK GUIDE

LESSON 8: GUT CHECK

Have you ever had that feeling that something wasn't quite right? I remember an incident that occurred at one of my past jobs. I was about to meet with a patient and the moment I stepped foot into the place, I wanted to turn around. However, I decided to shake it off and proceed with the meeting anyway. The closer I got to the meeting area, the more I wanted to turn around and *run*. This had never happened to me before in the 9 years I had been with this particular agency, so I wasn't sure why this was happening now.

Anyway, I finally met with the patient and began my session. As we talked, my hands became sweaty, my heart started pounding, and a voice in my head said, "Get out."

I wanted to get up right then, but I figured I could shake the feeling instead. I was the professional in this situation, so I didn't want to come off as afraid or intimidated. Besides, I wasn't quite sure why I was beginning to feel this way.

This was my first time meeting with this particular patient, and my instincts were reminding me all the reasons why I wished I had met him in my office first. In some cases, however, that's not always possible; especially when you are in the business of helping others. Thankfully, at the time, I hadn't received any negative reports or concerns regarding this patient and was told it was safe to meet with him outside of the office.

Before I meet with a patient, I always look up their history so that I am properly prepared, aware of my surroundings and can figure out an exit route if necessary. However, this time, none of that mattered. I was in a small room with the door shut. As I previously mentioned in the beginning, I am always observing peoples behaviorisms, tone of voice, facial expressions, etc.; and I was starting to panic. The look on this client's face concerned me.

"Get up and get out now!"

I tried to shrug it off, but the voice only grew louder in my head. I could see the monster slowly creeping up and showing itself through the client's eyes; there was a smirk on his face as if he had the upper hand in this situation. One jump from him and I would be pinned down. As every second went by, the harder and faster my heart was pounding. I could feel my body shaking.

"Get the hell out of here now!"

It felt like the longest five minutes ever. My body was starting to visibly shake through my skin. My papers were starting to shake, then, I looked at his eyes.

"Right now! Get up! Get up now! Before it's too late! Okay, calm down. Calm down. Oh Lord," is all I could tell myself.

I heard a noise behind the door and thought someone could be waiting to grab me. I feared for my life. I feared of possibly being attacked. I feared the unknown. Fortunately, I made up an excuse that I had forgot something at the office and had to leave right away. I then felt my body busting through the door and running to safety; but in reality, it appeared as though I simply got up and walked out. In that very moment, I had made up in my mind that the session was over. Unfortunately, everyone is not as lucky- or shall I say blessed- to make it out like I did.

Listen and Make the Right Moves

When your spirit tells you that something isn't right, listen. Some people may know that feeling and sometimes go with it, but then there are others who have not experienced it. In life and business, that gut feeling can save you. It can save your life, your business, your relationships, and your sanity. I had never experienced my gut feeling to be that strong, ever. Especially the moment I met the patient. This was a first. I knew then something was off but didn't know why I felt that way. On the outside people can look fine and act fine, but in their core, they can be evil.

Within the LONG, drawn out 5 minutes of meeting with that patient, I found out that he was one of the many that slipped through the cracks and needed way more intensive services than what I was trained to do. It definitely was not in the right setting and I definitely was not the one who he needed to meet with. Nothing but GOD protected me. When you hear that voice, that warning, and receive instructions and confirmation, you better move, especially if it's that crystal clear.

As an entrepreneur, you will meet many people and have many business deals. Some people you will be able to tell if they are genuine or just flat out bull-shitters. You may even get a slight feeling that something isn't right which will cause you to stay a little longer, search a little further, and even entertain a little longer. It's ok to walk away and not be 100% sure. At least you will still have your sanity and another day striving for greatness. But if you ignore that deep down gut feeling, it may cost you everything.

AN ENTREPRENEUR'S QUICK GUIDE

Lessons and Assignments

Lesson 8: Gut Check

When was the last time you listened or didn't listen to your gut feeling? What happened?

_____

_____

_____

_____

_____

_____

_____

_____

_____

_____

How did you feel after incident? And was it worth it?

_____

_____

_____

_____

_____

_____

_____

_____

_____

_____

Assignment: For the next month, do not rush into making a decision. Think everything out and write out the pros and cons before making decision.

Assignment: Every day, meditate at least 30 minutes to allow your inner self to guide you.

AN ENTREPRENEUR'S QUICK GUIDE

LIVING IN YOUR PURPOSE

Have you figured out what your purpose is? What do you love to do and how do you help others by doing it? If you couldn't get paid for it, would you still do it? Yes, I know that bills have to be paid and a lot of people don't do things for the *free*. However, let's hypothetically think of a perfect world where there are no bills or responsibilities: What would you be doing to help others for little to no pay? The gratification of knowing that you helped or provided resources to someone will help you identify what your true purpose is.

Always remember that your time, knowledge, and skills are valuable and to treat them as such. If others do not see the value in you, then you have to be okay with letting them go. If you can't let go, then dig deep and identify what's in you that is keeping you from living in your purpose and acknowledging your inner value. Who knows, the person or thing that you let go may come back to you with much greater appreciation and respect. Stop discounting yourself and your services for those who do not appreciate the exceptional quality that dwells in you and what you bring to the table.

In the meantime, get up and get to the grind. Nothing will be handed to you unless you have been born and raised with an unlimited amount of resources and money at your discretion. Are you amongst the top, wealthiest earners in the world?

Don't worry, I'll wait for your response.

But if you're like me, then join the club of hard working entrepreneurs and business owners.

You don't have to be perfect or have it all together. Just take that leap of faith and God will align everything you need in order for you to be successful. Even if it seems as if you are alone, broke, lost and confused, keep pushing and don't give up. The wolf in you will come out and help you elevate to the next level.

AN ENTREPRENEUR'S QUICK GUIDE

FINALS WORDS OF ADVICE

"Earn money. Start small and then work your way up." – Ti'jra, 7

"It's never too late to get started. You have to be dedicated." – Destinee, 16

"Have an idea for your business. Be willing to work that part of the business, and if you don't like it, then you should go back to the drawing board." – Darryl, 17

"No matter where you are on your journey, remember why you started." – Rachelle Clark, 26 (Co-Owner of MAW Supply)

"Do your research." – Delores Mouton, 65 (Retired Accounting Secretary)

"Be organized and have a to-do list. Always plan and never give up." – Antonia M. (Entrepreneur)

"Don't let fear hinder you from making your dreams or visions a reality. Believe in yourself and invest in self. We spend our lives building someone else's business. You have experience, skills and drive to make entrepreneurship a reality." – Nekeshia L. (Entrepreneur)

"Always do your research before jumping into anything. Never be the one to speak, always be the one to listen." – Stacey Simms, 46 (Senior Manager)

"You will fail over and over and over again. You will hit rock bottom so hard that you will want to quit. You will lose your friends. You will be exhausted. But if it's your passion, if you have a vision and not merely a dream, just keep pushing. Just keep going. Just keep trying. If you refuse to quit, you can't help but succeed." – Isaure Moorehead (Owner of IzzyMo Fitness & Nutrition, LLC)

"When starting your own business, be sure that you have reached deep into why you have created the business – why you enjoy it – how many lives you will touch with your business. A lot of times we have started a business concept that may already be in the market, and that's okay. You may have been given the gift to relate to people a certain way but with the same product. That's your 'why' and your niche! Also, when I say you have to enjoy it – that means when the going is good or when it's bad. Your enjoyment will be the extra reserve tank when you feel like you can't give anymore. Also, you need to realize that your business is not just about you – it's about the people you serve. Lastly, understand that the creator is a mastermind of relationship building and He connects you to everything and everyone you need." – Lawrence Brooks (Owner of Think Big Legacy Planning)

"Do your research. Have a mentor. Have money saved for opening and 6 months after. Never rely on one source of income." – Raychell Penns

(Author and Business Owner, Raychell Penns)

"If you really want to be a successful entrepreneur it's really simple: get started, make no excuses and starve your distractions! Nothing worth having comes easy. It will all be a part of your testimony in the end." – Jermaine A. (Entrepreneur)

"Starting a new journey as an entrepreneur is not about the end result. It's the path that you've embark to pursue your dream and vision. In order to be successful, look at your past failures and pursue your goals, with determination and persistence. It will not be easy, but keep striving because the sky has no limits. Work hard, stay positive and surround yourself with individuals who are positive influences. Lastly, don't accept

NO and I CAN'T as an answer. "- Deme Mars-Price (MBA)

Go ahead and LIVE IN YOUR PURPOSE. It's in you and waiting to burst out. Allow the wolf in you to come out and take a stand. It wil be and is worth the journey.

Thank you and I hope my Quick Guide was enjoyable and able to help you on this traveled path of life and entrepreneurial.

ABOUT THE AUTHOR

Cassandra Mouton, *MHRM, MBA*

Cassandra Mouton was born and raised in Houston, TX. in a single-parent home by the age of three, due to her father's unexpected death. Wanting to make a difference in the world, she continued and received her Bachelors in Social Work, Master's in Business Administration, and Masters in Human Resources with a concentration in Project Management.

In 2013, she became the founder and president of Touches of Art Inc., a non-profit 501(c) organization but has put that project on hold in order to persue other career goals.

She is the founder and president of A&D Management, LLC. A management and consulting company that has managed and consulted various federal, state, local, and non-profit projects.

Cassandra is now proud to say she has accomplished one of her goals, completing her first book entitled, *Pulling the Wolf Out of the Sheep: An Entrepreneur's Quick Guide and Workbook*. She has already started on her next book and checking off more things on her to do list.

She is a motivator, leader and inspiration to others. She thrives off of giving back to the community and humbly taking on the opportunities and challenges set before her. She is a woman of God, a loyal friend, and a dream chaser.

NOTES

NOTES

NOTES

NOTES

NOTES

NOTE

NOTES

NOTES

NOTES

NOTES

NOTES

NOTES

NOTES

ABOUT BY PUBLISHING

BY Publishing's mission is to give author's a strong Christian voice and platform to teach, speak and preach to the world.

We sincerely believe that you do not have to break the piggy bank to share your story with the world and become a bestselling author!

We provide a five-star signature, very inexpensive publishing, marketing, public relations and promotion service, we effectively assist authors to successfully publish and promote their life's works and truly connect to their friends, family and fans! We have a streamline system to launch you to a bestselling author.

Then the LORD answered me, "Write the vision. Make it clear on tablets so that anyone can read it quickly. Habakkuk 2:2

http://www.bypublishing.com